Henry A. Nelson

Benefits of the Sabbath

Henry A. Nelson

Benefits of the Sabbath

ISBN/EAN: 9783743325609

Manufactured in Europe, USA, Canada, Australia, Japa

Cover: Foto ©ninafisch / pixelio.de

Manufactured and distributed by brebook publishing software (www.brebook.com)

Henry A. Nelson

Benefits of the Sabbath

BENEFITS

OF THE

SABBATH.

BY
Rev. HENRY A. NELSON, D.D.

PHILADELPHIA:
PRESBYTERIAN PUBLICATION COMMITTEE,
1334 CHESTNUT STREET.
A. D. F. RANDOLPH, 770 BROADWAY, N. Y.

Entered according to Act of Congress, in the year 1867, by

WM. L. HILDEBURN, Treasurer,
in trust for the
PRESBYTERIAN PUBLICATION COMMITTEE,

In the Clerk's Office of the District Court for the Eastern District of Pennsylvania.

Westcott & Thomson,
Stereotypers, Philada.

BENEFITS OF THE SABBATH.

THE DAY OF REST.

The privilege of simply ceasing from labor, and *resting*, every seventh day, is a much greater privilege than it is apt to be regarded. It is a truth well established by experimental evidence, that, for the most perfect health of body and mind, and for the most successful continued labor, man as truly needs a weekly day of rest, as some hours of sleep every night. We do not say that the two are *equally* necessary. Doubtless a man can live longer without Sabbath rest than without nightly sleep. But he cannot enjoy the most perfect health without both; nor can he have so cheerful, nor probably so long a life.

This is evident from his own experience, to every thoughtful man accustomed to labor six days in the week. Is not every such man conscious of increasing weariness as the week advances? Does he not often feel that the draught upon his strength, made by the day's labor, is not quite made up by the night's repose? Does he not sometimes feel on Saturday evening as if he could not bear another day of toil? And after enjoying the Sabbath rest, does he not go to his work on Monday morning with a cheerfulness and a courage and a consciousness of renewed strength, such as he did not have on Saturday or Friday? This may not be the conscious experience of every week, but considering how often it is so, and considering what, at such times, would be the effect of continuing to labor on the Sabbath as on other days, we may well ask whether the system of the laborer would not run down without the Sabbath, like a clock without winding up?

A stated day of rest, respected by general custom, and held sacred, is better for this purpose than occasional holidays to be taken by each man at his discretion. It would be always difficult, and often impossible for the poor laborer to get such holidays. In many establishments, the arrangements made without reference to any stated days of rest, would render it impossible for laborers to be spared.

The fear of losing their places, and their natural reluctance to diminishing their earnings, would be always tempting them to hold on in continuous labor beyond the point of safe endurance. All the forces which, in such a case, would regulate employment and wages, would compel the poor to have as few holidays as possible. When we have duly considered all these things, we shall begin to see how kind and how efficient is the protection which God has given to the poor, in the institution of the Sabbath.

But they are not the poor only who are obliged to labor. They are not always the poorest who work hardest. Men who are accumulating wealth by successful business, and men who are distinguishing themselves in professional and public life, undergo more exhausting labor and are more familiar with depressing fatigue, than most of those who buy their daily food with the wages of their daily labor. How could you, men of business, do without the Sabbath? Could the constant stretch of your faculties which the demands of business occasion, be endured week after week without intermission? Do you know nothing of the experience already described,—

that increasing weariness as the week advances, that consciousness that the nightly rest is not enough for you, and that feeling on Saturday evening, that you have almost reached the limit of your capacity for exertion? Worn and jaded as you sometimes are at the end of a week, could you hold right on for another and another without any respite? Would it not soon make you a helpless invalid or a miserable maniac?

You, too, if left to find occasional holidays, would not be apt to find them often enough, nor when most needed. The pressure of competition, the urgency of customers kept away by no recognized usage, the sight and noise of business going on incessantly around you, the natural reluctance to sparing for rest time which would be as profitable as any for business,—all these things would tempt you to make your holidays as few as possible, and would make it impossible that any of them should yield you the undisturbed, refreshing repose, which is the rich gift of the Sabbath.

How well is it for you that the paternal voice of God calls you every seventh day to cease from all your labors, and hushes the world about you to a friendly stillness, and gives you permission, retreating within the safe enclosures of your home and of His Sanctuary, to shut out all the demands of business from your attention, and without discourtesy to forbid all the calls of business upon you.

This matter has been tested by experiment. Mankind have not all had faith enough in the wisdom and goodness of their Maker to keep His commandments without trying the experiment whether they could prosper without a Sabbath. Some serious, observing, thinking persons, have carefully made large collections of facts from the experience of such people. Those facts show most conclusively that both men and beasts actually do more work in a year, or any number of years, working only six days in each week, than if they work all the seven days. They also show that those who habitually labor on the Sabbath, the same as on other days, experience the same decay of bodily vigor, the same gradual undermining of the physical constitution, and the same deterioration of the mental powers, as those who are habitually prevented from enjoying sufficient rest at night.

Most evidently, He who made man, He

by whose hands this bodily frame was so curiously wrought, and by whose skill this marvellous connection of our bodies and souls was established, instituted the Sabbath in view of what he so well knew of the wants of our nature. "*The Sabbath was made for man.*"

VALUABLE HABITS PROMOTED BY THE SABBATH.

The Sabbath is friendly to some of the most useful habits. We name, as specimens, *cleanliness, order,* and *punctuality.*

All well-informed physiologists assure us that sound health, serenity, cheerfulness of temper, and vigor of intellect are greatly dependent upon habitual bodily *cleanliness.* This physiological truth is of great practical importance. A clean skin and clean linen are capital preservers of health. Every scholar ought to know that without these he is never in a good state for successful study. Such cleanliness has also an important moral influence. If you carefully study the ceremonial law of the Old Testament, and if you duly consider the figurative terms by which the Bible describes moral purity, you will be convinced that in the estimation of the Divine

Author of that Book and that Ritual, there is no slight connection between bodily cleanliness and purity of mind. And if you are attentive to your own experiences, you will not fail to discover that it is easiest to keep the mind free from evil and open to good influences when the body and its clothing are cleanest. Now a glance at any assembly of Sabbath worshippers will show that their observance of the Sabbath strongly promotes this desirable habit. Those who frequent Christian sanctuaries always have enough of regard for the God who is there worshipped, or for the feelings of fellow-worshippers, or enough self-respect to take some pains to go there, and to see that their children go clean, and in clean, (though it may be cheap and homely), apparel.

Order in the discharge of our duties and in the division of our time is greatly assisted by the Sabbath. It divides our time into periods of convenient length for the going through with many circles of duties. This is very manifest in respect to household duties. In good and orderly house-keeping, each day of the week has its appropriate labor. All housewives will probably agree that that necessary circle of labors could not well be completed in fewer days than six; and all tidy and thrifty housewives will say that no one of these labors could well be intermitted for a longer time. But it is not so much that the week is of just the right length, as that without the Sabbath we should have *no week at all.* Each week is a definite period, having accurate limits, and separated from the period next to it by a sacred day, into which your week-day affairs may not be carried. You therefore require yourself to finish up those affairs within the prescribed period. In order that the week's work may be finished within the week, it is requisite that each day's duties be done within that day. This arrangement of time furnishes strong inducements and many facilities for bringing all kinds of business affairs to a frequent and periodical settlement. You try to keep your matters so adjusted that you can close them all up every Saturday night, and lay them by without damage. Orderly habits are much more easily maintained than they could be, if all the days ran on in an unbroken series, without any distinction between them.

Punctuality is so closely allied to order

that, if that is promoted by the Sabbath this cannot fail to be promoted also. Certainly the habit of planning to complete every week's work within the week, and in order to this to do each day's work within its day, cannot but be favorable to habits of punctuality. Though this is a rare virtue, it is a most important one, and the guardian of many others. The man who is never late, who never keeps another waiting for him, who never delays nor interrupts proceedings at which he should be present by late attendance, shows genuine honesty,—honesty which as much disdains to pilfer time as money. If such a man should never accomplish any great thing, he at least may have the comfort of reflecting that he has not hindered others from accomplishing what they were able to do. Blessed be the man who is never waited for. It is no small thing that God, by his division of time into weeks, has given so much aid and encouragement to this important virtue.

Having thus illustrated the tendency of the Sabbath to promote these good habits, I must satisfy myself with the suggestion that what is so favorable to these cannot fail to be favorable to the whole family of virtues to which they belong. I have no doubt that the observation of my readers, in whatever direction it may be extended, will justify the suggestion. When we see the Sabbath thus encouraging and nourishing the virtuous habits on which the happiness of mankind is so dependent, must we not make a very high estimate of its value?

SOCIAL ENJOYMENT.

There is a kind of social enjoyment appropriate to the Sabbath, and for which the Sabbath affords the most favorable opportunities; and it is the best and purest we can have in this world. I refer to that society which is found within the limits of the family circle. Consider how many heads of families can be at home very little except on the Sabbath. A mechanic, whose employment generally kept him away from home during the week, and who had lately suffered the severest of domestic bereavements, bewailed his widowed state in the following touching strain:—

"A year ago, when Saturday came, I would be often counting the hours that must pass before my week's work would be finished, and I could go home to my family. And when at length the happy hour came, I would gather up my tools and take my homeward way with a glad heart. My wife always welcomed me with an affectionate smile, and I was made comfortable and happy by her kind attentions. On the Sabbath morning she was always ready to go to church with me, and for fifteen years she stood up by my side in the choir, almost every Sabbath, and we sang the praises of God together. But now, when my week's work is finished, and I am ready to go home, I have to recollect that I have no home. I go to my boarding-place, and though the family show me every possible kindness, I still pass a lonely evening. On Sabbath-day I have to go to church alone, and stand up alone to sing. *She* is not by my side, and *her* voice does not mingle with mine."

This honest man's simple story touches our hearts. It is a pitiful sight to see a fellow-man thus bereaved, a human home thus broken up. But for our support under such sorrow there are strong consolations provided. The Sabbath itself brings the most healing influences to hearts thus torn. From the Sanctuary God sends the most effectual help to such sufferers. So the afflicted man felt whose words have been cited. He sorrows not without hope nor without comfort. But if it be such an affliction to have customary Sabbath privileges thus interrupted, what a calamity would it be to the thousands of such men to have their Sabbath wholly taken from them! What a sorrowful abatement would it be from the happiness of such families, if there were no week's end at which the husband and father could come home to them,— no Sabbath which he could spend with them!

My readers are familiar with that beautiful poem of Burns, "The Cotter's Saturday Night." Could any thing on this earth furnish the scene for so lovely a picture, if there were no Sabbath? That poem truthfully describes the Saturday evening of many a Scottish cottage; and there is not more of poetic ardor than of sober truth in the poet's exclamation,—

"From scenes like these old Scotia's grandeur springs,
That makes her loved at home, revered abroad."

There are thousands of humble happy homes in our country in which the Saturday evening exhibits similar scenes,—where a happiness so serene, so pure, so heavenly, descends upon the gathered family. How many hearts turn, in later life, with fondest recollections, to the kind greetings, the cheerful converse, the warbling of sacred songs in harmony of heart and voice, the patriarchal counsels, and the fervent prayer of such Saturday evenings! What would become of all this if we had no Sabbath? What have they of all this who observe no Sabbath?

Here, as before, it is not only the poor who partake of the blessing. How little, except on Sabbaths, are business men with their families? Ye merchants and bankers, ye men of commerce and traffic, would not the very faces of your children grow strange to you, if you had not this one day in the week to be with them, enjoying such intercourse as best cultivates their affection for you, and imparting to them such lessons of instruction as are fitted to form them to a character of virtue and piety? You perhaps have not the Saturday evening for such enjoyment. That may be your most toilsome evening. It is to be regretted that the business customs of our time crowd so hard upon the confines of the

Sabbath. But it is a great blessing that at least from the midnight hour preceding the Sabbath, you may say to the pressing tide of worldliness, "*Thus far—no farther.*" Although you may retire weary and late on Saturday night, you wake on Sabbath morning with the pleasant consciousness of freedom. You feel that, on that day, no urgency of business may encroach upon your retirement. On that day you may have some hours to spend in the guarded quiet of home, in the society of your family, enjoying the purest and sweetest pleasures. We need this day of rest for the refreshment of our hearts as well as our bodies and our intellects—not more for the repose of our physical energies, than for the happiest exercise and culture and quiet growth of our choicest affections.

MORAL INFLUENCE.

We speak of the Sabbath, not merely as a day of rest from labor, not merely a holiday, but as a sacred day; a day set apart peculiarly for the worship of God and the contemplation of divine things, and the systematic communication of religious instruction, for reading the Holy Scriptures, and instructing the young out of them, and preaching the Gospel. Incalculable is the influence which, by these means, the Sabbath sends forth upon the community, restraining men from crime, reclaiming them from vicious habits, keeping them from temptations to sensuality, prompting them to enterprises of public utility, correcting and elevating the public sentiment and improving and evangelizing the public spirit. It is plain, from the most common observation, that those places in which the Sabbath is not regarded, and in which there is no Sanctuary, are the places in which crime and vice most abound, and there is the least of virtuous order and virtuous sentiment. There the people are the most grovelling, and the most rude, and the most addicted to demoralizing and debasing practices. Generally speaking, it is to the men and women who frequent the Sanctuary, and religiously keep the Sabbath, that we must look, under God, to uphold the great interests of morality and virtue in any community.

Says Chalmers:—"The suspension, on this day, of the labor and business of the world, its scrupulous retirement from the converse or the festivities of common intercourse, its solemn congregations, and its evening solitude—these singly and in themselves, may not be esteemed as moralities, and yet be entitled to a high pre-eminence among them, from the impulse they give to that living fountain of piety, out of which the various moralities of life ever come forth in purest and most plenteous emanation. It is not that the virtue of man consists in these things, but that these things are devices of best and surest efficacy for upholding the virtue of man. * * * And you have only to compute the worth and the celestial character of all those graces which have been sheltered, and fed, and reared to maturity, in the bosom of this institution, that you may own the high bearing and dignity which belong to it."

If there is any man who doubts the value of the Sabbath in this respect, we would propose to him to go to some place where there is no Sanctuary, and where none of the people have any regard for the Sabbath, and after remaining long enough to learn the real character of the people, and to ascertain the full amount of securities, of which he could there avail himself, for his property and life and personal rights, to come back and tell us whether he is disposed to make a home there for his family. Nay, there is not a place on earth, where there is no Sabbath, in which one of our readers would be willing to live. The Sabbath is indeed the great upholder of all those moral virtues which are essential to the peace and security and order of human society.

OUR ETERNAL WELFARE.

The Sabbath has a prominent, a commanding position in the system of agencies by which the salvation of human souls is secured. It is the truth that is preached in the Sanctuary, and for the devout contemplation of which the Sabbath affords the best opportunities, which God employs as the chief means of renewing and sanctifying the soul; and it is upon the Sabbath in the Sanctuary, that the greatest numbers of God's people unite in those fervent supplications, in answer to which He sends down His saving influences most abundantly upon the hearts of men. With all our natural worldliness, all our readiness to forget God and disregard our eternal interests, if we were left in this world without any Sabbath, how few of us would ever be prepared for heaven! This is immeasurably the most important of all the benefits of the Sabbath. For this especially it is given to us, that we may have a good and favorable opportunity to hear the Gospel, and to consider its proposals, and to meditate on its sanctifying truth, and to enjoy its edifying ordinances, and so to "work out our salvation," God working in us with His efficient energy, by means of His appointed and hallowed instrumentalities.

The temporal interests upon which we have seen that the Sabbath exerts so favorable an influence, (though they be the most precious of temporal interests), are trifles in comparison with this, and except as they are subsidiary and preliminary to this. They are the incidental benefits which result from setting up, in the world, an institution, the chief purpose of which relates to eternity. So it is always. "Godliness is profitable unto all things, having promise of the life that now is and of that which is to come." Whatever tends to secure our eternal well-being, helps us to be happy here. Whatever helps the people of this world to prepare for a residence in heaven, fails not to bring down something of the blessedness of heaven into this world. He who lay down to sleep where, in his dream, he saw a ladder set upon the earth, the top of which reached unto heaven, had the angels for visitors, and from above the ladder the voice of God came down to him promising the most abundant blessings to him and to his seed. So always they enjoy the best blessings which can be possessed in this world, who dwell nearest to the sacred pathways which lead up to heaven.

The Sabbath justly claims the regard due to an institution which, rightly used, will procure for us the best earthly blessings, and afford us the best opportunities for securing eternal happiness.

Some practical reflections are naturally suggested by the view which we have taken of the benefits of the Sabbath.

1. We have reason to give thanks continually to God for an institution which He has made the vehicle for conveying to us so many of His choicest blessings, and to which He has given power to shed influences so benign upon human society. If we give thanks for peace and good order prevailing in our communities, we should remember the influence

of the Sabbath in promoting them. If we acknowledge the goodness of God in securing abundant and steady rewards to honest labor, we should also thank Him for the refreshment and blessing of the day of rest, and that this rest is so extensively enjoyed by the poorest and the most laborious of our people. Grateful for civil and religious liberty, we should not forget that the Sabbath is our liberty's principal safeguard; that no people have long enjoyed stable and orderly liberty who were not enlightened and sobered by Sabbath observance. And when we offer thanks for the infinite blessings of the Gospel, we cannot fail to praise God for that sacred day upon which we hear its glad sound unmingled with the din of this world's business, and whose guarded retirement and solemn services are so well suited to open our hearts to its tender and earnest appeals. Let us praise the Lord that He has instituted the Sabbath for the benefit of mankind, and that He has given us our descent from an ancestry upon which, for so many ages, the hallowed influences of the Sabbath have descended.

2. The obligation to honor the Sabbath and faithfully to observe it, is made more plain

by this consideration of its benefits. "*Remember the Sabbath day to keep it holy.*" The solemn commandment comes to us with augmented force, from the large experience which mankind have had of the value of the Sabbath. The blessings which it will confer upon any people, must also be proportioned to the fidelity with which they keep it. Let us be careful not to let the business of the world encroach upon it, and let us endeavor to be always prepared for the devout contemplations to which it invites, and to receive and improve the good influences of which it is the source.

3. We cannot forget that a large number of our countrymen are cruelly deprived of Sabbath rest and Sabbath privileges. While Christians in the country walk or ride to their houses of worship on the pleasant summer Sabbaths, or quietly sit in their pews attending to the Gospel, or enjoy Sabbath repose at home, they must know that on the canals, thousands of friendless boys, (some of them orphan sons of departed Christians), are plodding on in unrespited toil, toil that prematurely wears out the body, and sadly debases the mind. On the great rivers, a numerous

host of laborers are held in equally wretched servitude, slaves of a commerce which enriches the country, and supplies us with abundant means of living in comfort and luxury, conducted on a system which assumes the moral degradation of its menials and effectually ensures it by making Sabbath privileges impossible. Directing and superintending these, and conducting the business of this immense navigation, are a great number of men higher in the intellectual and social scale, many of whom carry unquiet consciences until they get them benumbed and callous, obliged by this Sabbath-breaking system to choose between this violation of their consciences and the immediate loss of their only means of self-support, and too generally yielding to the temptation, to the conscious debasement of their manhood and the peril of their souls.

In many cities, the new street-railway system employs a great number of drivers and conductors, whose situation is a monstrous anomaly. Kept on duty a greater number of hours than any other laborers, and required to work on Sabbaths as on other days, they get no respite from toil except the hours of nightly sleep. If a man in such employment

BENEFITS OF THE SABBATH.

be the father of a family, and if his little children have the amount of sleep which healthful childhood needs, he can never see them awake, unless it be while hastily snatching his mid-day meal, if haply he can run to his home in the short time allotted to that. His children may outgrow their capacity for enjoying paternal fondling without ever having an opportunity to sit upon his knees. Meantime his car may rumble by the doors of more than one Sanctuary, and halt for the accommodation of their worshippers every Sabbath day, and he never hear a sermon, or a psalm, or a prayer.

There are other classes, whose business as it is conducted in many branches, and usages of society which we too thoughtlessly permit to prevail, and legislation unworthy of a Christian nation, compel to forego the rest and the benefits of the Sabbath. Society cannot thus rob a part of its members of their most sacred privileges, and constrain them to such moral debasement without suffering in all its interests. One of our most prosperous and eminent merchants of New York, a director of one of the longest and most important railroads in our country, endeavoring to persuade his fellow-directors to let their road rest on Sunday, made this shrewd remark to them, "If you will compel your conductors to break the fourth commandment, you have no right to expect that they will keep the eighth." He did not, we presume, mean to affirm that every man who will work on Sunday will steal; but doubtless he did mean, that a company whose arrangements exclude from their employ all men of *first-class consciences*, must expect to find a large per-centage of its employees not very scrupulous in handling its money. Doubtless this is true. That director made a just and rational estimate of the pecuniary hazard of disregarding God's commandment, which doubtless he would keep irrespective of such considerations. In like manner, everywhere and in all relations, important interests are imperilled, and corruption and moral depravation are induced by arrangements which constrain men to violate the Sabbath.

Our national Government is yet far from setting a worthy example in this respect. A numerous class of its most loyal and law-abiding citizens are excluded from employment in some of the most important branches of the public service, because they could not hold such places without working on the Sabbath. By this means, the probabilities are increased, that such trusts will fall into the hands of unscrupulous men, and the influence of the Government is brought to bear directly upon young men to diminish their conscientiousness, and thus to corrupt and destroy them. What harm or loss could result from the entire stopping of the mails and closing of the Post Offices during the hours of the Sabbath, at all comparable with the harm and loss of making Post Office employment a grand corrupter of young men's consciences, and a grand weakener of the divine safeguard of public virtue? When transportation is so easy and swift, and the transmission of important intelligence can be effected instantaneously, can we not agree to let the multitude of men employed in this department of public service, enjoy the rest of the Sabbath? Do we not want a Sabbath blessing upon our common medium of social and commercial intercommunication? May we not hope, by vigorous, continuous, and candid discussion, to bring this American people to see that only by being a Sabbath-keeping people can they secure the blessing which they most highly prize?

God grant that the time may come when the Sabbath will be universally regarded; when from its dawn to its close no government office will be open, nor any public business transacted; when no Congress will ever let the work of legislation encroach upon its sacred hours; when every railroad depot will be silent; every locomotive motionless; every steamboat moored, and its cabin or deck made a Sanctuary; when every laborer will have his right to the weekly season of rest secured to him; when every inhabitant of our wide and populous land will dwell within hearing of a Sabbath bell, and be disposed to accept its significant invitation; when from free and enlightened pulpits the Word of God shall be proclaimed in its purity to all the people, and all the hallowed influences of the Sabbath shall be exerted in every dwelling, upon the hearts of every family. Then shall we be a truly happy people. Then shall we "delight ourselves in the Lord, and He will cause us to ride upon the high places of the earth, and feed us with the heritage of

Jacob,"—even the rich heritage of His everlasting covenant. Then "God, even our own God, shall bless us. God shall bless us, and all the ends of the earth shall fear Him."

THE END.